Published in paperback in 2014 by Wayland
Text copyright © Pat Thomas 2014
Illustrations copyright © Lesley Harker 2014

Wayland
Hachette Children's Books
338, Euston Road,
London NW1 3BH

Wayland Australia
Level 17/207 Kent Street
Sydney, NSW 2000

Concept design: Kate Buxton
Series design: Elaine Wilkinson

British Library Cataloguing in Publication Data
Thomas, Pat, 1959-
Everybody Matters : a first look at respect for others. --
(A first look at)
1. Respect for persons--Juvenile literature.
2. Friendship--Juvenile literature.
I. Title II. Series
158.2-dc22

First published in 2010 by Wayland

ISBN: 978 0 7502 8864 4

Printed in China

Wayland is a division of Hachette Children's Books,
an Hachette UK company.
www.hachette.co.uk

Everybody Matters

A FIRST LOOK AT RESPECT FOR OTHERS

PAT THOMAS
ILLUSTRATED BY LESLEY HARKER

WAYLAND

You have probably heard people use the word 'respect'. But do you know what respect means?

Respect is a little word,
with a very big meaning.

7

Respect is a word we use
to talk about lots of
different feelings
all at once.

Feelings like trust, friendship, love, faith,
and, maybe most of all, equality.

When you respect someone you see them as your equal, as being just as good as you are.

When you think of someone in this way, you pay more attention to the ways in which you are alike...

...and don't worry too much about the ways in which you are different.

Most of the differences
between human beings
are ones we can see
with our eyes.

What makes us alike are the
things we feel in our hearts.

There are some types of respect that we all deserve.

Like being treated fairly, not being called names or shouted at...

...and not being made fun of because we are different.

And there are some types of respect that we have to earn
by doing things like keeping our promises, being loyal,
being polite, listening, and being honest with others.

The more you show respect to others by doing these things, the more they will respect you in return.

What about you?

Can you think of some ways you can show respect to others?
Are there other things like animals and plants that need
our respect as well?

Some people think they can force
others to respect them...

...and some think they deserve respect even when they
haven't done anything to earn it.

These people act like bullies, and
try to scare people into doing
what they tell them to do.

But being scared of someone isn't the
same as respecting them.

Because when you are scared you feel like the other person is bigger, or better, or more powerful than you.

Respect always makes you feel that you are as important as anyone else.

Showing respect doesn't mean never disagreeing.

Everyone is entitled to their own feelings and opinions –
even if they are different from other people's.

If you respect someone you try to understand why they think or believe something – even if you don't think or believe it yourself.

Sometimes you just have to agree to disagree!

What about you?

Can you think of some times that you didn't agree with someone?
Can you think of ways to show someone that you respect them,
even if you disagree with them?

Everybody wants respect, but not everybody knows how to show it.

We all have to practise showing respect every day –
even grown ups...

...because the more you practise, the better you get at it.

And when we all try to respect each other, and treat each other as equals...

...our homes and schools – and even our world – become happier places for us all to work and play and live together.

HOW TO USE THIS BOOK

Modern culture has skewed the notion of respect drastically in recent years. Through TV, films and music, children learn that respect is something they receive, or are somehow 'owed', but rarely do they learn that it is something that needs to be given to others. Showing respect for others is certainly more complicated than demanding it for yourself. It can often involve a complicated set of social skills that take years to master. Parents need to make the effort to teach respect in a deliberate, intentional way since the more positive reinforcement the message gets at home, the more deeply the lesson will be learned.

Parents are a child's first teachers and role models. And showing respect for your child is probably the best way to begin. You can do this by using kind words, helping when you can, sharing, listening to what others have to say, being honest and truthful, thinking before you speak and act, practising good manners, controlling your temper, thinking about the feelings of others, and applying the principles of fairness at home and at work.

Self-respect is an important form of respect, since once we respect ourselves, it is easier to respect others. A child who feels valued for who they are, and who has been helped to learn self respect takes care of him or herself, their belongings and responsibilities in a conscientious way, will find it easier to respect others.

Likewise, help your child to know that respect is more than avoiding conflict. It doesn't mean that people never lose their tempers or act impulsively. It means that people know how to talk to each other, appreciate each other's differences and have a basic willingness to co-operate and compromise. Let children know that sometimes the most respectful solution is to 'agree to disagree'. Not all conflicts can be resolved. But that doesn't mean that we can't respect each other and live and work peacefully side by side.

In a multicultural society respect is crucial. There are many ways to teach appreciation of diversity. Encourage open discussions at home about the ways in which we are all different and the ways in which we are all the same. In modern society, we mix and match many aspects of other cultures, for instance in what we eat, how we dress, the music we listen to. (English in particular borrows words from many different languages.) Point these out to your child as examples of 'common ground' with other cultures.

Schools are ideal places to help teach respect, tolerance and appreciation of diversity. Most of the time this is done indirectly, for instance by celebrating the holidays and festivals of many cultures and teaching about the traditions and foods of different cultures. Where possible teachers may wish to be more direct.

To emphasize the point that different people have different likes and dislikes, teachers can invite children to share something - a food, an activity, a place, or anything else - they like very much. After everyone has shared, ask some of the students to identify things that other students like but they don't like as much. This discussion is a good way to show that people should treat one another respectfully in spite of their differences.

BOOKS TO READ

Values: I Don't Care!: Learning about Respect
Brian Moses (Wayland, 1998)

All Kinds of People: a Lift-the-Flap Book
Emma Damon (Tango Books, 1995)

All Kinds of Beliefs: a Lift-the-Flap Book
Emma Damon (Tango Books, 2000)

Helping Polly Parrot! Pirates can be kind
Tom Easton and Mike Gordon (Wayland 2014)

Don't Call Me Special: A first look at disability
Pat Thomas (Wayland 2014)

This is My Family: A first look at same-sex parents
Pat Thomas (Wayland, 2014)

RESOURCES FOR ADULTS

Respect! Exploring Children's Rights in the UK and Around the World
Save the Children (Save the Children, 2008)

Respect (Adventures from the Book of Virtues)
(Golden Books Publishing Company, 1998)

Hands Around the World: 365 Creative Ways to Build Cultural Awareness and Global Respect
Susan Milford (Williamson Publishing Co, 1992)